Addition

no regrouping

H.S. Lawrence

Illustration by
Kathy Kifer and Dahna Solar

Special thanks to:
Jane Troy, Holly Dye, Derrick Hoffman, Mercedes Diaz, Gerry Turman,
Andrea & Suzanne Adelman, and Cecily Cleveland

Published by
Garlic Press
100 Hillview Lane #2
Eugene, OR 97401

ISBN 0-931993-49-0
Order Number GP-049

Overview: Math and Animal Science

The Puzzles and Practice Series builds basic **math skills** and acquaints students with **animal science**. The Series is also designed to challenge skills associated with following directions, simple logic, visual discrimination (all puzzle assembly skills), and motor skills (cutting and pasting).

Practice Pages illustrate math skills step-by-step, then provide extended practice. **Puzzle Pages** contain twelve-piece puzzles that when assembled reveal a fascinating animal. This book in the Series features Endangered Species.

Endangered Species Reference Cards, found on the last three pages of this book, provide further information for students. In addition, for parents and teachers, the inside front cover provides **background information** on Endangered Species.

Helping Teachers and Parents

There are two pages for each of the twelve lessons- a Practice Page and a Puzzle Page. Each page can be used independently; however, the Puzzles and Practice Series has incorporated a special feature that encourages the use of both pages at one time.

Special Feature- If you hold a *Puzzle Page* up to the light, you will see the same problems showing in the center of the puzzle pieces (actually showing through from the *Practice Page*) that are to the left of the puzzle pieces on the Puzzle Page. This feature is useful so a student will not lose the potential for the answer after he or she has cut out the puzzle piece. This feature is also useful if a student does not follow directions and cuts out all puzzle pieces at one time.

Table of Contents

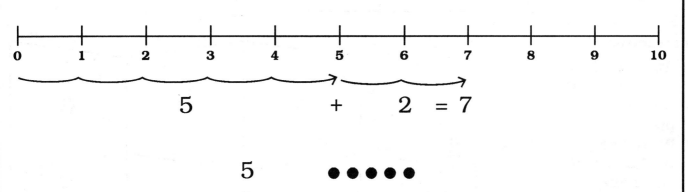

$$5 + 2 = 7$$

$$\begin{array}{r} 5 \\ + 2 \\ \hline 7 \end{array}$$

$$\begin{array}{r} 2 \\ + 3 \\ \hline \end{array} \quad \begin{array}{r} 0 \\ + 4 \\ \hline \end{array} \quad \begin{array}{r} 2 \\ + 8 \\ \hline \end{array} \quad \begin{array}{r} 1 \\ + 0 \\ \hline \end{array} \quad \begin{array}{r} 6 \\ + 1 \\ \hline \end{array} \quad \begin{array}{r} 0 \\ + 0 \\ \hline \end{array} \quad \begin{array}{r} 3 \\ + 6 \\ \hline \end{array} \quad \begin{array}{r} 5 \\ + 1 \\ \hline \end{array}$$

$$\begin{array}{r} 0 \\ + 1 \\ \hline \end{array} \quad \begin{array}{r} 7 \\ + 2 \\ \hline \end{array} \quad \begin{array}{r} 4 \\ + 3 \\ \hline \end{array} \quad \begin{array}{r} 5 \\ + 5 \\ \hline \end{array} \quad \begin{array}{r} 2 \\ + 1 \\ \hline \end{array} \quad \begin{array}{r} 4 \\ + 4 \\ \hline \end{array} \quad \begin{array}{r} 3 \\ + 2 \\ \hline \end{array} \quad \begin{array}{r} 1 \\ + 4 \\ \hline \end{array}$$

$$\begin{array}{r} 2 \\ + 0 \\ \hline \end{array} \quad \begin{array}{r} 1 \\ + 3 \\ \hline \end{array} \quad \begin{array}{r} 7 \\ + 1 \\ \hline \end{array} \quad \begin{array}{r} 3 \\ + 4 \\ \hline \end{array} \quad \begin{array}{r} 2 \\ + 2 \\ \hline \end{array} \quad \begin{array}{r} 9 \\ + 0 \\ \hline \end{array} \quad \begin{array}{r} 3 \\ + 3 \\ \hline \end{array} \quad \begin{array}{r} 3 \\ + 7 \\ \hline \end{array}$$

$$\begin{array}{r} 0 \\ + 0 \\ \hline \end{array} \quad \begin{array}{r} 4 \\ + 2 \\ \hline \end{array} \quad \begin{array}{r} 8 \\ + 1 \\ \hline \end{array} \quad \begin{array}{r} 2 \\ + 6 \\ \hline \end{array} \quad \begin{array}{r} 6 \\ + 4 \\ \hline \end{array} \quad \begin{array}{r} 1 \\ + 1 \\ \hline \end{array} \quad \begin{array}{r} 5 \\ + 3 \\ \hline \end{array} \quad \begin{array}{r} 1 \\ + 2 \\ \hline \end{array}$$

NAME
NOMBRE _____

Instructions:

1. **Answer all the math problems first.**
2. **Cut out one puzzle piece at a time.**
3. **Paste the puzzle piece in the box with the same answer.**

Instrucciones:

1. Conteste todos los problemas de matemáticas primero.
2. Recorte una pieza del rompecabezas a la vez.
3. Pegue la pieza del rompecabezas en el recuadro que tiene la misma respuesta.

GRIZ
E L O

5	0	6
3	7	4	8

3	7	4	8
1	9	2	10

$$\begin{array}{r} 3 \\ + 2 \\ \hline \end{array}$$

$$\begin{array}{r} 2 \\ + 1 \\ \hline \end{array}$$

$$\begin{array}{r} 4 \\ + 3 \\ \hline \end{array}$$

$$\begin{array}{r} 0 \\ + 1 \\ \hline \end{array}$$

$$\begin{array}{r} 3 \\ + 3 \\ \hline \end{array}$$

$$\begin{array}{r} 2 \\ + 2 \\ \hline \end{array}$$

$$\begin{array}{r} 7 \\ + 1 \\ \hline \end{array}$$

$$\begin{array}{r} 2 \\ + 0 \\ \hline \end{array}$$

$$\begin{array}{r} 6 \\ + 4 \\ \hline \end{array}$$

$$\begin{array}{r} 8 \\ + 1 \\ \hline \end{array}$$

$$\begin{array}{r} 0 \\ + 0 \\ \hline \end{array}$$

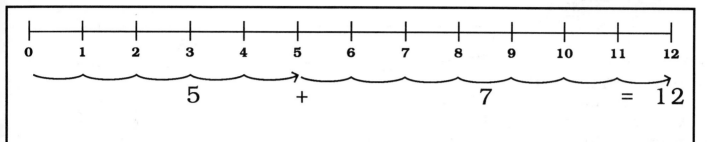

$$5 + 7 = 12$$

$$\begin{array}{r} 5 \\ + 7 \\ \hline 12 \end{array}$$

3 + 4	9 + 2	1 + 1	5 + 3	12 + 0	2 + 4	7 + 2	5 + 6
1 + 5	3 + 6	6 + 6	8 + 3	0 + 2	2 + 5	3 + 1	6 + 2
2 + 1	9 + 3	6 + 1	1 + 4	7 + 3	3 + 0	5 + 4	3 + 3
7 + 4	2 + 8	4 + 4	5 + 7	0 + 1	6 + 4	2 + 3	2 + 2

NAME
NOMBRE _____

Instructions:

1. **Answer all the math problems first.**
2. **Cut out one puzzle piece at a time.**
3. **Paste the puzzle piece in the box with the same answer.**

Instrucciones:

1. Conteste todos los problemas de matemáticas primero.
2. Recorte una pieza del rompecabezas a la vez.
3. Pegue la pieza del rompecabezas en el recuadro que tiene la misma respuesta.

2	1	7	8
4	5	9	11
3	12	6	10

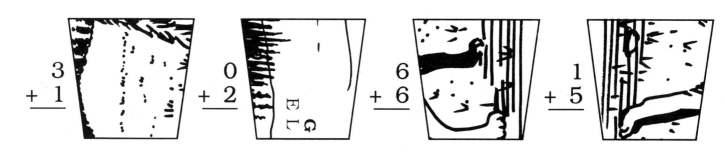

$$\begin{array}{r} 3 \\ +\ 1 \\ \hline \end{array}$$
$$\begin{array}{r} 0 \\ +\ 2 \\ \hline \end{array}$$
$$\begin{array}{r} 6 \\ +\ 6 \\ \hline \end{array}$$
$$\begin{array}{r} 1 \\ +\ 5 \\ \hline \end{array}$$

$$\begin{array}{r} 5 \\ +\ 4 \\ \hline \end{array}$$
$$\begin{array}{r} 7 \\ +\ 3 \\ \hline \end{array}$$
$$\begin{array}{r} 6 \\ +\ 1 \\ \hline \end{array}$$
$$\begin{array}{r} 2 \\ +\ 1 \\ \hline \end{array}$$

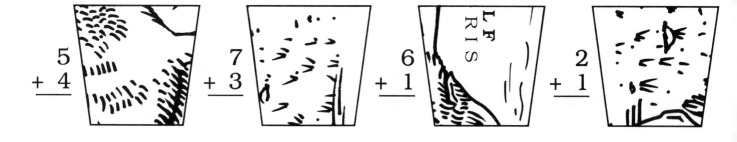

$$\begin{array}{r} 2 \\ +\ 3 \\ \hline \end{array}$$
$$\begin{array}{r} 0 \\ +\ 1 \\ \hline \end{array}$$
$$\begin{array}{r} 4 \\ +\ 4 \\ \hline \end{array}$$
$$\begin{array}{r} 7 \\ +\ 4 \\ \hline \end{array}$$

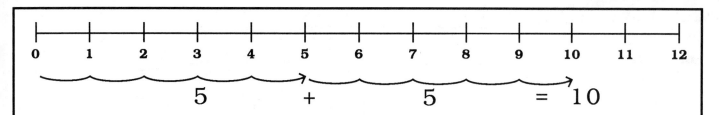

$$\begin{array}{r} 5 \\ + 5 \\ \hline 10 \end{array}$$

$$\begin{array}{r} 1 \\ + \square \\ \hline 1 \end{array} \quad \begin{array}{r} 4 \\ + \square \\ \hline 12 \end{array} \quad \begin{array}{r} 9 \\ + \square \\ \hline 10 \end{array} \quad \begin{array}{r} 1 \\ + \square \\ \hline 7 \end{array} \quad \begin{array}{r} 4 \\ + \square \\ \hline 8 \end{array} \quad \begin{array}{r} 3 \\ + \square \\ \hline 11 \end{array} \quad \begin{array}{r} 7 \\ + \square \\ \hline 10 \end{array} \quad \begin{array}{r} 5 \\ + \square \\ \hline 12 \end{array}$$

$$\begin{array}{r} 1 \\ + \square \\ \hline 3 \end{array} \quad \begin{array}{r} 8 \\ + \square \\ \hline 8 \end{array} \quad \begin{array}{r} 3 \\ + \square \\ \hline 8 \end{array} \quad \begin{array}{r} 7 \\ + \square \\ \hline 11 \end{array} \quad \begin{array}{r} 2 \\ + \square \\ \hline 9 \end{array} \quad \begin{array}{r} 4 \\ + \square \\ \hline 7 \end{array} \quad \begin{array}{r} 3 \\ + \square \\ \hline 12 \end{array} \quad \begin{array}{r} 2 \\ + \square \\ \hline 11 \end{array}$$

$$\begin{array}{r} 1 \\ + \square \\ \hline 4 \end{array} \quad \begin{array}{r} 6 \\ + \square \\ \hline 12 \end{array} \quad \begin{array}{r} 5 \\ + \square \\ \hline 11 \end{array} \quad \begin{array}{r} 7 \\ + \square \\ \hline 8 \end{array} \quad \begin{array}{r} 2 \\ + \square \\ \hline 10 \end{array} \quad \begin{array}{r} 1 \\ + \square \\ \hline 8 \end{array} \quad \begin{array}{r} 0 \\ + \square \\ \hline 1 \end{array} \quad \begin{array}{r} 5 \\ + \square \\ \hline 10 \end{array}$$

$$\begin{array}{r} 7 \\ + 5 \\ \hline \square \end{array} \quad \begin{array}{r} 5 \\ + \square \\ \hline 5 \end{array} \quad \begin{array}{r} 4 \\ + 6 \\ \hline \square \end{array} \quad \begin{array}{r} 5 \\ + \square \\ \hline 7 \end{array} \quad \begin{array}{r} 8 \\ + 3 \\ \hline \square \end{array} \quad \begin{array}{r} 4 \\ + \square \\ \hline 9 \end{array} \quad \begin{array}{r} 2 \\ + 2 \\ \hline \square \end{array} \quad \begin{array}{r} 3 \\ + \square \\ \hline 5 \end{array}$$

NAME
NOMBRE _____

Instructions:

1. Answer <u>all</u> the math problems first.
2. Cut out <u>one</u> puzzle piece at a time.
3. Paste the puzzle piece in the box with the same answer.

Instrucciones:

1. Conteste <u>todos</u> los problemas de matemáticas primero.
2. Recorte <u>una</u> pieza del rompecabezas a la vez.
3. Pegue la pieza del rompecabezas en el recuadro que tiene la misma respuesta.

$8 + 3 = \square$ $4 + 2 = \square$ $3 + 0 = \square$ $8 + 2 = \square$

$5 + 2 = \square$ $1 + 1 = \square$ $1 + 4 = \square$ $3 + 5 = \square$

$0 + 1 = \square$ $3 + 6 = \boxed{9}$ $9 + 3 = \square$ $2 + 2 = \square$

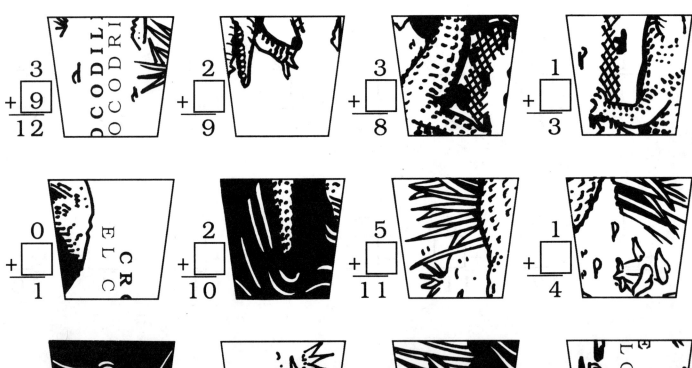

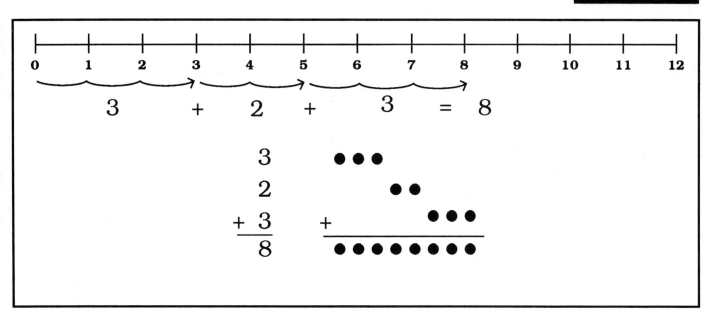

$$3 + 2 + 3 = 8$$

```
  3
  2
+ 3
———
  8
```

```
  0      6      2      3      0      1      2      0
  2      1      1      2      0      2      1      0
+ 3    + 4    + 5    + 7    + 2    + 1    + 4    + 0
```

```
  1      1      0      3      5      3      2      3
  2      0      1      1      1      2      3      5
+ 3    + 3    + 2    + 4    +6     + 1    + 4    +1
```

```
  2      5      0      2      1      3      6      4
  3      3      1      3      0      1      2      0
+ 3    + 3    + 4    + 2    + 1    + 1    + 3    + 2
```

```
  2      7      3      2      1      2      0      1
  6      4      1      3      1      5      1      1
+ 2    + 1    + 3    + 5    + 2    + 2    + 0    + 1
```

NAME
NOMBRE _____

Instructions:

1. **Answer all the math problems first.**
2. **Cut out one puzzle piece at a time.**
3. **Paste the puzzle piece in the box with the same answer.**

Instrucciones:

1. Conteste todos los problemas de matemáticas primero.
2. Recorte una pieza del rompecabezas a la vez.
3. Pegue la pieza del rompecabezas en el recuadro que tiene la misma respuesta.

2	10	12	6
4	9	8	5
3	11	7	1

$$\begin{array}{r} 2 \\ 3 \\ +\ 4 \\ \hline \end{array}$$

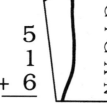
$$\begin{array}{r} 5 \\ 1 \\ +\ 6 \\ \hline \end{array}$$

$$\begin{array}{r} 0 \\ 1 \\ +\ 2 \\ \hline \end{array}$$

$$\begin{array}{r} 1 \\ 2 \\ +\ 3 \\ \hline \end{array}$$

$$\begin{array}{r} 6 \\ 2 \\ +\ 3 \\ \hline \end{array}$$

$$\begin{array}{r} 1 \\ 0 \\ +\ 1 \\ \hline \end{array}$$

$$\begin{array}{r} 0 \\ 1 \\ +\ 4 \\ \hline \end{array}$$

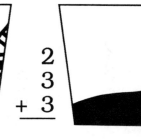
$$\begin{array}{r} 2 \\ 3 \\ +\ 3 \\ \hline \end{array}$$

$$\begin{array}{r} 0 \\ 1 \\ +\ 0 \\ \hline \end{array}$$

$$\begin{array}{r} 1 \\ 1 \\ +\ 2 \\ \hline \end{array}$$

$$\begin{array}{r} 3 \\ 1 \\ +\ 3 \\ \hline \end{array}$$

$$\begin{array}{r} 2 \\ 6 \\ +\ 2 \\ \hline \end{array}$$

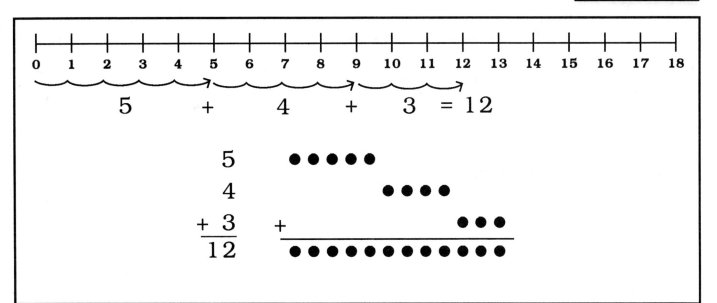

$$5 + 4 + 3 = 12$$

| |
| 5 |
| 4 |
| + 3 |
| 12 |

```
  8      4      6      1      5      4      5      3
  3      8      1      2      2      3      0      5
+ 2    + 6    + 9    + 2    + 4    + 7    + 1    + 4
```

```
  2      4      6      7      1      3      2      6
  3      5      2      3      6      2      7      9
+ 5    + 6    + 4    + 7    +8     + 2    + 9    + 2
```

```
  7      9      6      8      9      5      1      8
  1      2      2      1      3      3      4      2
+ 3    + 5    + 6    + 2    + 5    + 6    + 4    + 5
```

```
  9      2      3      1      1      0      0      1
  0      1      8      6      2      7      4      3
+ 4    + 4    + 5    + 5    + 5    +6     + 3    + 6
```

NAME
NOMBRE _____

Instructions:

1. **Answer all the math problems first.**
2. **Cut out one puzzle piece at a time.**
3. **Paste the puzzle piece in the box with the same answer.**

Instrucciones:

1. Conteste todos los problemas de matemáticas primero.
2. Recorte una pieza del rompecabezas a la vez.
3. Pegue la pieza del rompecabezas en el recuadro que tiene la misma respuesta.

```
  6        5      4        9
+ 6      + 8    + 5      + 9


  7      2        1      2
+ 7    + 9      + 7    + 5


  9        7    6        8
+ 8      + 8  + 4      + 8
```

```
  2
  7
+ 9
```

```
  1
  6
+ 8
```

```
  6
  2
+ 4
```

```
  2
  3
+ 5
```

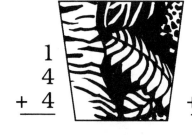
```
  1
  4
+ 4
```

```
  9
  3
+ 5
```

```
  6
  2
+ 6
```

```
  7
  1
+ 3
```

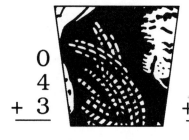
```
  0
  4
+ 3
```

```
  3
  8
+ 5
```

```
  1
  2
+ 5
```

```
  9
  0
+ 4
```

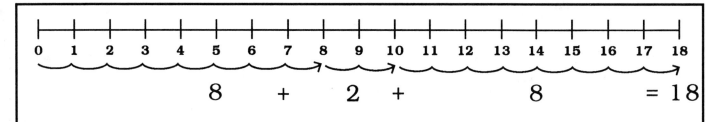

$$8 + 2 + 8 = 18$$

8 ●●●●●●●●

2 ●●

$\begin{array}{r}8\\2\\+\ 8\\\hline 18\end{array}$ ●●●●●●●●

+ ─────────────

●●●●●●●●●●●●●●●●●●

| $\begin{array}{r}2\\\boxed{\ }\\+\ 5\\\hline 8\end{array}$ | $\begin{array}{r}3\\\boxed{\ }\\+\ 6\\\hline 17\end{array}$ | $\begin{array}{r}1\\\boxed{\ }\\+\ 1\\\hline 12\end{array}$ | $\begin{array}{r}7\\\boxed{\ }\\+\ 2\\\hline 16\end{array}$ | $\begin{array}{r}9\\\boxed{\ }\\+\ 0\\\hline 10\end{array}$ | $\begin{array}{r}3\\\boxed{\ }\\+\ 5\\\hline 14\end{array}$ | $\begin{array}{r}1\\\boxed{\ }\\+\ 4\\\hline 8\end{array}$ | $\begin{array}{r}3\\\boxed{\ }\\+\ 8\\\hline 15\end{array}$ |

| $\begin{array}{r}4\\6\\+\boxed{\ }\\\hline 10\end{array}$ | $\begin{array}{r}1\\\boxed{\ }\\+\ 1\\\hline 11\end{array}$ | $\begin{array}{r}7\\7\\+\boxed{\ }\\\hline 17\end{array}$ | $\begin{array}{r}3\\\boxed{\ }\\+2\\\hline 13\end{array}$ | $\begin{array}{r}2\\4\\+\boxed{\ }\\\hline 11\end{array}$ | $\begin{array}{r}5\\\boxed{\ }\\+\ 7\\\hline 14\end{array}$ | $\begin{array}{r}9\\1\\+\boxed{\ }\\\hline 18\end{array}$ | $\begin{array}{r}4\\\boxed{\ }\\+\ 3\\\hline 13\end{array}$ |

| $\begin{array}{r}2\\1\\+\boxed{\ }\\\hline 12\end{array}$ | $\begin{array}{r}3\\\boxed{\ }\\+\ 9\\\hline 17\end{array}$ | $\begin{array}{r}3\\4\\+\boxed{\ }\\\hline 14\end{array}$ | $\begin{array}{r}8\\\boxed{\ }\\+\ 4\\\hline 16\end{array}$ | $\begin{array}{r}5\\2\\+\boxed{\ }\\\hline 9\end{array}$ | $\begin{array}{r}4\\\boxed{\ }\\+\ 8\\\hline 18\end{array}$ | $\begin{array}{r}0\\5\\+\boxed{\ }\\\hline 15\end{array}$ | $\begin{array}{r}1\\\boxed{\ }\\+\ 5\\\hline 16\end{array}$ |

| $\begin{array}{r}4\\\boxed{\ }\\+\ 6\\\hline 11\end{array}$ | $\begin{array}{r}2\\\boxed{\ }\\+\ 2\\\hline 9\end{array}$ | $\begin{array}{r}7\\0\\+\boxed{\ }\\\hline 8\end{array}$ | $\begin{array}{r}5\\\boxed{\ }\\+\ 7\\\hline 15\end{array}$ | $\begin{array}{r}3\\9\\+\boxed{\ }\\\hline 18\end{array}$ | $\begin{array}{r}3\\\boxed{\ }\\+\ 6\\\hline 9\end{array}$ | $\begin{array}{r}8\\1\\+\boxed{\ }\\\hline 13\end{array}$ | $\begin{array}{r}5\\\boxed{\ }\\+\ 3\\\hline 10\end{array}$ |

NAME
NOMBRE _____

Instructions:

1. **Answer <u>all</u> the math problems first.**
2. **Cut out <u>one</u> puzzle piece at a time.**
3. **Paste the puzzle piece in the box with the same answer.**

Instrucciones:

1. Conteste <u>todos</u> los problemas de matemáticas primero.
2. Recorte <u>una</u> pieza del rompecabezas a la vez.
3. Pegue la pieza del rompecabezas en el recuadro que tiene la misma respuesta.

0	7	6	3
8	1		5
10	4	9	2

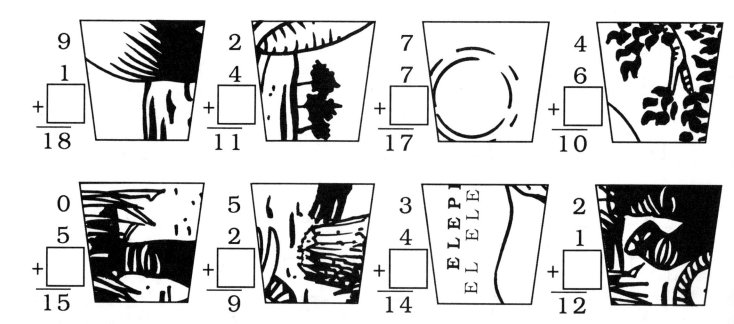

$$\begin{array}{r} 9 \\ 1 \\ +\ \square \\ \hline 18 \end{array}$$

$$\begin{array}{r} 2 \\ 4 \\ +\ \square \\ \hline 11 \end{array}$$

$$\begin{array}{r} 7 \\ 7 \\ +\ \square \\ \hline 17 \end{array}$$

$$\begin{array}{r} 4 \\ 6 \\ +\ \square \\ \hline 10 \end{array}$$

$$\begin{array}{r} 0 \\ 5 \\ +\ \square \\ \hline 15 \end{array}$$

$$\begin{array}{r} 5 \\ 2 \\ +\ \square \\ \hline 9 \end{array}$$

$$\begin{array}{r} 3 \\ 4 \\ +\ \square \\ \hline 14 \end{array}$$

$$\begin{array}{r} 2 \\ 1 \\ +\ \square \\ \hline 12 \end{array}$$

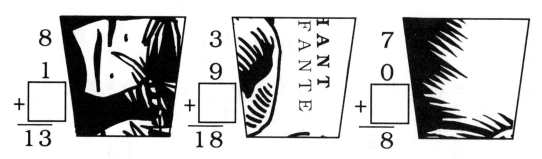

$$\begin{array}{r} 8 \\ 1 \\ +\ \square \\ \hline 13 \end{array}$$

$$\begin{array}{r} 3 \\ 9 \\ +\ \square \\ \hline 18 \end{array}$$

$$\begin{array}{r} 7 \\ 0 \\ +\ \square \\ \hline 8 \end{array}$$

NAME
NOMBRE _____

$$53 \rightarrow \begin{array}{r} 5\boxed{3} \\ + \boxed{4} \\ \hline \boxed{7} \end{array} \rightarrow \begin{array}{r} \boxed{5}3 \\ + \boxed{}4 \\ \hline \boxed{5}7 \end{array} \rightarrow \begin{array}{r} 53 \\ + 4 \\ \hline 57 \end{array}$$

$$\begin{array}{r} 71 \\ + 1 \\ \hline \end{array} \qquad \begin{array}{r} 92 \\ + 4 \\ \hline \end{array} \qquad \begin{array}{r} 25 \\ + 2 \\ \hline \end{array} \qquad \begin{array}{r} 33 \\ + 3 \\ \hline \end{array} \qquad \begin{array}{r} 51 \\ + 8 \\ \hline \end{array} \qquad \begin{array}{r} 83 \\ + 2 \\ \hline \end{array} \qquad \begin{array}{r} 31 \\ + 3 \\ \hline \end{array} \qquad \begin{array}{r} 15 \\ + 4 \\ \hline \end{array}$$

$$\begin{array}{r} 42 \\ + 3 \\ \hline \end{array} \qquad \begin{array}{r} 24 \\ + 2 \\ \hline \end{array} \qquad \begin{array}{r} 31 \\ + 7 \\ \hline \end{array} \qquad \begin{array}{r} 43 \\ + 4 \\ \hline \end{array} \qquad \begin{array}{r} 24 \\ + 5 \\ \hline \end{array} \qquad \begin{array}{r} 34 \\ + 3 \\ \hline \end{array} \qquad \begin{array}{r} 12 \\ + 6 \\ \hline \end{array} \qquad \begin{array}{r} 53 \\ + 5 \\ \hline \end{array}$$

$$\begin{array}{r} 82 \\ + 5 \\ \hline \end{array} \qquad \begin{array}{r} 62 \\ + 1 \\ \hline \end{array} \qquad \begin{array}{r} 71 \\ + 6 \\ \hline \end{array} \qquad \begin{array}{r} 52 \\ + 2 \\ \hline \end{array} \qquad \begin{array}{r} 64 \\ + 4 \\ \hline \end{array} \qquad \begin{array}{r} 72 \\ + 7 \\ \hline \end{array} \qquad \begin{array}{r} 55 \\ + 1 \\ \hline \end{array} \qquad \begin{array}{r} 36 \\ + 3 \\ \hline \end{array}$$

$$\begin{array}{r} 42 \\ +6 \\ \hline \end{array} \qquad \begin{array}{r} 11 \\ + 4 \\ \hline \end{array} \qquad \begin{array}{r} 26 \\ + 1 \\ \hline \end{array} \qquad \begin{array}{r} 42 \\ + 0 \\ \hline \end{array} \qquad \begin{array}{r} 33 \\ + 6 \\ \hline \end{array} \qquad \begin{array}{r} 75 \\ + 3 \\ \hline \end{array} \qquad \begin{array}{r} 97 \\ + 2 \\ \hline \end{array} \qquad \begin{array}{r} 73 \\ + 1 \\ \hline \end{array}$$

NAME
NOMBRE _____

Instructions:

1. Answer <u>all</u> the math problems first.
2. Cut out <u>one</u> puzzle piece at a time.
3. Paste the puzzle piece in the box with the same answer.

Instrucciones:

1. Conteste <u>todos</u> los problemas de matemáticas primero.
2. Recorte <u>una</u> pieza del rompecabezas a la vez.
3. Pegue la pieza del rompecabezas en el recuadro que tiene la misma respuesta.

18	68	77	27
39	56	38	48
99	45	29	87

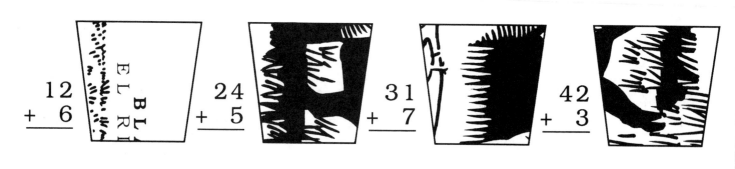

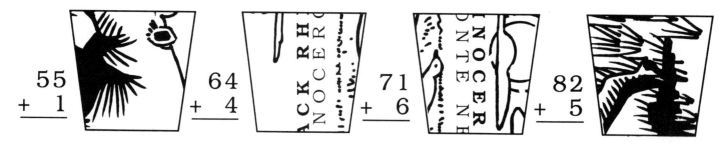

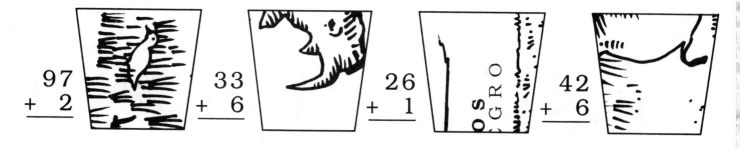

NAME
NOMBRE _____

$$\begin{array}{r} 42 \\ +\ 5 \\ \hline \end{array} \rightarrow \begin{array}{r} 4\boxed{\begin{array}{c}2 \\ 5 \\ \hline 7\end{array}} \\ + \end{array} \rightarrow \begin{array}{r} \boxed{\begin{array}{c}42 \\ +\ 5 \\ \hline 4\end{array}}7 \\ \end{array} \rightarrow \begin{array}{r} 42 \\ +\ 5 \\ \hline 47 \end{array}$$

50	46	24	74	91	34	54	61
+ 6	+ 3	+ 3	+ 2	+ 7	+ 1	+ 5	+ 2

31	43	53	93	22	93	71	84
+ 4	+ 5	+ 1	+ 1	+ 7	+ 2	+ 3	+ 4

81	62	76	40	31	83	22	25
+ 8	+ 5	+ 2	+ 5	+ 6	+ 3	+ 2	+ 3

42	31	97	21	52	43	62	73
+ 4	+ 1	+ 0	+ 5	+ 6	+ 4	+ 3	+ 6

NAME
NOMBRE _____

Instructions:

1. **Answer all the math problems first.**
2. **Cut out one puzzle piece at a time.**
3. **Paste the puzzle piece in the box with the same answer.**

Instrucciones:

1. Conteste todos los problemas de matemáticas primero.
2. Recorte una pieza del rompecabezas a la vez.
3. Pegue la pieza del rompecabezas en el recuadro que tiene la misma respuesta.

70 + 4 = ___	80 + 9 = ___	60 + 5 = ___	20 + 4 = ___
30 + 5 = ___	20 + 9 = ___	30 + 7 = ___	40 + 6 = ___
50 + 8 = ___	90 + 7 = ___	70 + 8 = ___	50 + 4 = ___

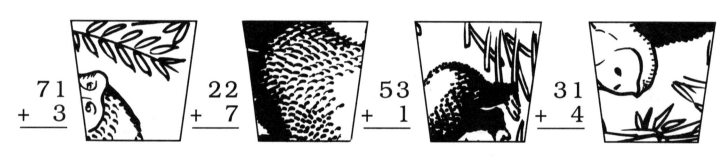

$$\begin{array}{r} 71 \\ +\ 3 \\ \hline \end{array} \qquad \begin{array}{r} 22 \\ +\ 7 \\ \hline \end{array} \qquad \begin{array}{r} 53 \\ +\ 1 \\ \hline \end{array} \qquad \begin{array}{r} 31 \\ +\ 4 \\ \hline \end{array}$$

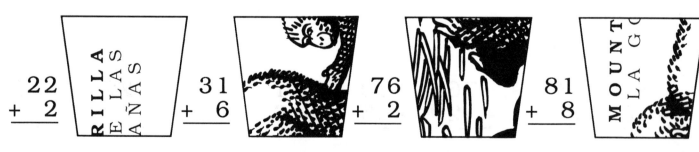

$$\begin{array}{r} 22 \\ +\ 2 \\ \hline \end{array} \qquad \begin{array}{r} 31 \\ +\ 6 \\ \hline \end{array} \qquad \begin{array}{r} 76 \\ +\ 2 \\ \hline \end{array} \qquad \begin{array}{r} 81 \\ +\ 8 \\ \hline \end{array}$$

$$\begin{array}{r} 62 \\ +\ 3 \\ \hline \end{array} \qquad \begin{array}{r} 52 \\ +\ 6 \\ \hline \end{array} \qquad \begin{array}{r} 97 \\ +\ 0 \\ \hline \end{array} \qquad \begin{array}{r} 42 \\ +\ 4 \\ \hline \end{array}$$

NAME
NOMBRE _____

$$
\begin{array}{r} 6\,1 \\ +2\,3 \\ \hline \end{array}
\quad\rightarrow\quad
\begin{array}{r} 6\,1 \\ +2\,3 \\ \hline \mathbf{4} \end{array}
\quad\rightarrow\quad
\begin{array}{r} 6\,1 \\ +2\,3 \\ \hline \mathbf{8}\,4 \end{array}
\quad\rightarrow\quad
\begin{array}{r} 6\,1 \\ +2\,3 \\ \hline 8\,4 \end{array}
$$

13 +65	11 +10	30 +62	73 +11	53 +26	25 +22	46 +32	84 +15
34 +62	23 +50	12 +46	61 +26	15 +24	38 +30	41 +23	15 +34
12 +22	11 +14	32 +37	12 +70	26 +31	51 +16	20 +15	45 +41
35 +21	42 +32	74 +24	20 +17	23 +42	14 +41	13 +84	71 +10

NAME
NOMBRE _____

Instructions:

1. **Answer all the math problems first.**
2. **Cut out one puzzle piece at a time.**
3. **Paste the puzzle piece in the box with the same answer.**

Instrucciones:

1. Conteste todos los problemas de matemáticas primero.
2. Recorte una pieza del rompecabezas a la vez.
3. Pegue la pieza del rompecabezas en el recuadro que tiene la misma respuesta.

98	39	65	34
64	97	58	96
57	35	69	56

$$41 + 23$$ $$15 + 24$$ $$12 + 46$$ $$34 + 62$$

$$20 + 15$$ $$26 + 31$$ $$32 + 37$$ $$12 + 22$$

$$13 + 84$$ $$23 + 42$$ $$74 + 24$$ $$35 + 21$$

NAME
NOMBRE _____

```
 60  →   60  →   60  →   60
+25     +25     +25     +25
         5       85      85
```

25	73	31	20	24	34	53	74
+20	+14	+35	+74	+65	+42	+30	+24

22	13	30	23	39	61	68	47
+15	+36	+56	+32	+60	+23	+11	+12

16	17	24	20	53	27	12	23
+12	+22	+51	+60	+43	+40	+21	+24

13	54	41	53	25	16	48	10
+10	+23	+27	+42	+33	+81	+40	+80

NAME
NOMBRE _____

Instructions:

1. Answer all the math problems first.
2. Cut out one puzzle piece at a time.
3. Paste the puzzle piece in the box with the same answer.

Instrucciones:

1. Conteste todos los problemas de matemáticas primero.
2. Recorte una pieza del rompecabezas a la vez.
3. Pegue la pieza del rompecabezas en el recuadro que tiene la misma respuesta.

46 +40	48 +10	28 +60	38 +30
27 +10	79 +20	23 +10	18 +10
66 +30	35 +40	39 +40	13 +10

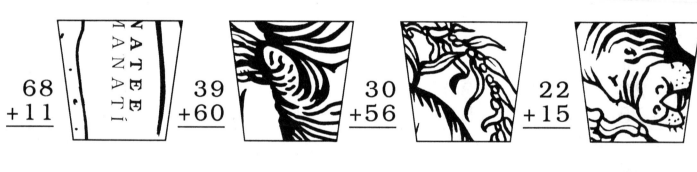

68
+11

39
+60

30
+56

22
+15

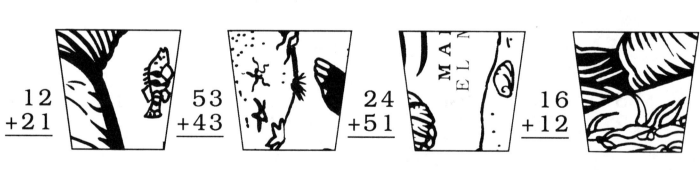

12
+21

53
+43

24
+51

16
+12

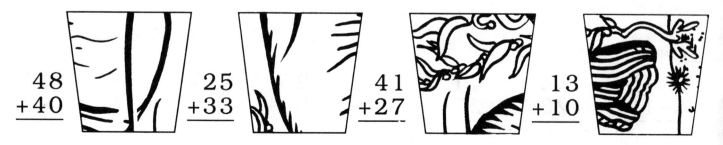

48
+40

25
+33

41
+27

13
+10

NAME
NOMBRE _____

```
  15  →   1⎡5⎤  →   ⎡1⎤5  →    15
  22      2⎢2⎥      ⎢2⎥2        22
 +31     +3⎣1⎦     ⎣3⎦1       +31
         ──────    ──────     ─────
           8         68         68
```

12	21	40	31	12	11	40	13
10	50	24	15	10	30	40	63
+11	+20	+20	+31	+43	+11	+13	+10

13	31	52	25	41	27	11	11
42	20	13	11	36	11	22	22
+21	+44	+24	+43	+10	+20	+33	+10

60	24	21	24	62	21	10	32
17	21	16	21	13	11	11	20
+22	+12	+11	+24	+23	+16	+12	+12

16	10	14	16	32	21	10	11
12	21	25	42	14	10	13	14
+11	+10	+20	+30	+21	+46	+15	+72

NAME
NOMBRE _____

Instructions:

1. Answer <u>all</u> the math problems first.
2. Cut out <u>one</u> puzzle piece at a time.
3. Paste the puzzle piece in the box with the same answer.

Instrucciones:

1. Conteste <u>todos</u> los problemas de matemáticas primero.
2. Recorte <u>una</u> pieza del rompecabezas a la vez.
3. Pegue la pieza del rompecabezas en el recuadro que tiene la misma respuesta.

13 +25	26 +41	32 +27	17 +22
23 +10	32 +66	21 +27	43 +56
32 +34	43 +44	25 +64	23 +53

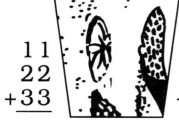
11
22
+33

41
36
+10

52
13
+24

13
42
+21

10
11
+12

62
13
+23

21
16
+11

60
17
+22

10
13
+15

32
14
+21

14
25
+20

16
12
+11

NAME
NOMBRE _____

```
26  →   26   →   26   →   26
31       31       31       31
+32      +32      +32      +32
          9        89       89
```

14	52	13	12	24	30	52	14
24	13	26	74	20	13	11	13
+21	+22	+40	+12	+25	+12	+13	+10

14	13	21	10	25	13	33	60
31	12	16	20	32	24	33	10
+20	+11	+20	+11	+32	+31	+33	+20

50	21	11	11	12	31	12	11
34	35	41	20	51	42	22	16
+12	+32	+12	+11	+14	+20	+12	+11

17	12	21	32	10	21	22	14
30	41	10	22	65	17	34	31
+11	+30	+13	+12	+10	+10	+22	+30

NAME
NOMBRE _____

Instructions:

1. **Answer <u>all</u> the math problems first.**
2. **Cut out <u>one</u> puzzle piece at a time.**
3. **Paste the puzzle piece in the box with the same answer.**

Instrucciones:

1. Conteste <u>todos</u> los problemas de matemáticas primero.
2. Recorte <u>una</u> pieza del rompecabezas a la vez.
3. Pegue la pieza del rompecabezas en el recuadro que tiene la misma respuesta.

57	78	44	99
46	65	85	64
89	96	58	77

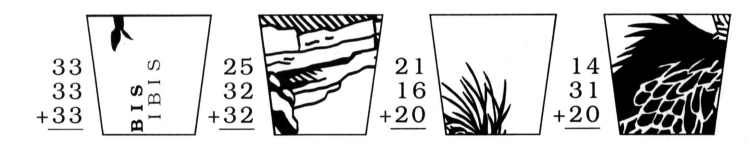

```
 33        25        21        14
 33        32        16        31
+33       +32       +20       +20
```

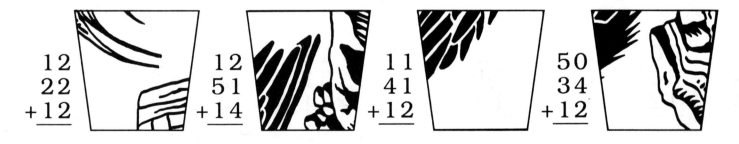

```
 12        12        11        50
 22        51        41        34
+12       +14       +12       +12
```

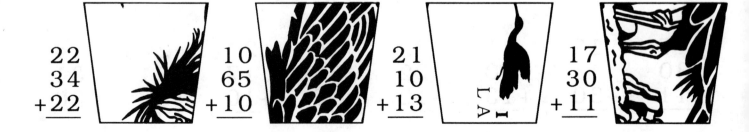

```
 22        10        21        17
 34        65        10        30
+22       +10       +13       +11
```

NAME
NOMBRE _____

```
 61   ○64        93   ○95        62   ○68        83   ○85
+ 2   ●63       + 2   ○94       + 5   ○66       + 3   ○86
─────  ○65       ────  ○96       ────  ○67       ────  ○87
 63
```

```
  3   ○10         2   ○10         9   ○11         6   ○ 9
+ 6   ○ 9       + 8   ○ 9       + 3   ○13       + 4   ○11
────  ○ 8       ────  ○11       ────  ○12       ────  ○10
```

```
 13   ○59        61   ○94        53   ○95        23   ○67
+36   ○49       +23   ○85       +42   ○96       +54   ○79
────  ○48       ────  ○84       ────  ○85       ────  ○77
```

```
  4   ○15         1   ○11         2   ○17         3   ○14
  5   ○17         6   ○13         7   ○16         4   ○15
+ 6   ○16       + 5   ○12       + 9   ○18       + 6   ○13
────            ────            ────            ────
```

```
 31   ○85        27   ○58        61   ○87        21   ○82
 20   ○95        11   ○59        24   ○99        10   ○62
+44   ○96       +20   ○68       +12   ○97       +41   ○72
────            ────            ────            ────
```

25

Answers

Lessons 1 - 12 & Post Test

Page 1.

5	4	10	1	7	0	9	6
1	9	7	10	3	8	5	5
2	4	8	7	4	9	6	10
0	6	9	8	10	2	8	3

Page 3.

7	11	2	8	12	6	9	11
2	9	12	11	2	7	4	8
3	12	7	5	10	3	9	6
11	10	8	12	1	10	5	4

Page 5.

0	8	1	6	4	8	3	7
2	0	5	4	7	3	9	9
3	6	6	1	8	7	1	5
12	0	10	2	11	5	4	2

Page 7.

5	11	8	12	2	4	7	0
6	4	3	8	12	6	9	9
8	11	5	7	2	5	11	6
10	12	7	10	4	9	1	3

Page 9.

13	18	16	5	11	14	6	12
10	15	12	17	15	7	18	17
11	16	14	11	17	14	9	15
13	7	16	12	8	13	7	10

Page 11.

1	8	10	7	1	6	3	4
0	9	3	8	5	2	8	6
9	5	7	4	2	6	10	10
1	5	1	3	7	0	4	2

Page 13.

72	96	27	36	59	85	34	19
45	26	38	47	29	37	18	58
87	63	77	54	68	79	56	39
48	15	27	42	39	78	99	74

Page 15.

56	49	27	76	98	35	59	63
35	48	54	94	29	95	74	88
89	67	78	45	37	86	24	28
46	32	97	26	58	47	65	79

Page 17.

78	21	92	84	79	47	78	99
96	73	58	87	39	68	64	49
34	25	69	82	57	67	35	86
56	74	98	37	65	55	97	81

Page 19.

45	87	66	94	89	76	83	98
37	49	86	55	99	84	79	59
28	39	75	80	96	67	33	47
23	77	68	95	58	97	88	90

Page 21.

33	91	84	77	65	52	93	86
76	95	89	79	87	58	66	43
99	57	48	69	98	48	33	64
39	41	59	88	67	77	38	97

Page 23.

59	87	79	98	69	55	76	37
65	36	57	41	89	68	99	90
96	88	64	42	77	93	46	38
58	83	44	66	85	48	78	75

Page 25 - Post Test

63	95	67	86
9	10	12	10
49	84	95	77
15	12	18	13
95	58	97	72

Grizzly Bear

Found in the United States.

Endangered!

Grizzly Bears are killed for their claws and for their gall bladders which are used to make medicines.

El Oso Gris

Se encuentran en los Estados Unidos.

¡En Peligro de Extinción!

Los osos grises se matan para sus garras y su vesícula biliar que se usa para hacer medicina.

Grey Wolf

Found in Canada and the United States (North America).

Endangered!

Ranchers and farmers kill the grey wolf to stop them from killing their animals.

El Lobo Gris

Se encuentran en Canadá y en los Estados Unidos (Norteamérica).

¡En Peligro de Extinción!

Los rancheros y los agricultores matan a los lobos grises para evitar que matan a sus animales.

Crocodile

Found in North America, South America, Africa, and Asia.

Endangered!

The leather skin of the crocodile is used to make clothing and goods. Swamps and wetlands are cleared by people who want to live there.

El Cocodrilo

Se encuentran en Norteamérica, Sudamérica, Africa y Asia.

¡En Peligro de Extincíon!

La piel de cuero del cocodrilo se usa para hacer ropa y mercancías. Las personas están despejando los pantanos y las tierras mojadas porque quieren vivir allí.

Giant Panda

Found in China.

Endangered!

Pandas have beautiful fur. Hunters hunt them to sell their fur.

El Panda Gigante

Se encuentran en China.

¡En Peligro de Extincíon!

Los pandas tienen piel muy bella. Los cazadores los matan para vender la piel.

Tiger

Found in Asia.

Endangered!

Ranchers and farmers kill tigers to stop them from killing their animals.

El Tigre

Se encuentran en Asia.

¡En Peligro de Extinción!

Los rancheros y los agricultores matan a los tigres para evitar que maten a sus animales.

Elephant

Found in Africa and Asia.

Endangered!

Ivory tusks are valuable. Hunters kill elephants and sell the tusks.

El Elefante

Se encuentran en Africa y en Asia.

¡En Peligro de Extinción!.

Los colmillos de marfil tienen mucho valor. Los cazadores matan a los elefantes y venden los colmillos.

Black Rhinoceros

Found in Africa.

Endangered!

The horns of the rhinoceros are worth money. People kill them and sell the horns.

El Rinoceronte Negro

Se encuentran en Africa.

¡En Peligro de Extinción!

Los cuernos del rinoceronte valen mucho dinero. Las personas los matan y venden los cuernos.

Mountain Gorilla

Found in Africa.

Endangered!

Adult gorillas are killed by hunters. Jungle homes are being cleared away by people wanting to live there.

El Gorila de las Montañas

Se encuentran en Africa.

¡En Peligro de Extinción!

Los cazadores matan a los gorilas adultos. Las personas están despejando sus hogares en la selva porque quieren vivir allí.